Ready
Text Collection

4000350927

PEARSON

Glenview, Illinois • Boston, Massachusetts • Chandler, Arizona • Hoboken, New Jersey

Cover: Chris Dickason

ISBN-13: 978-0-328-85797-5
ISBN-10:   0-328-85797-1
4 16

Knowing About Patterns and Structures

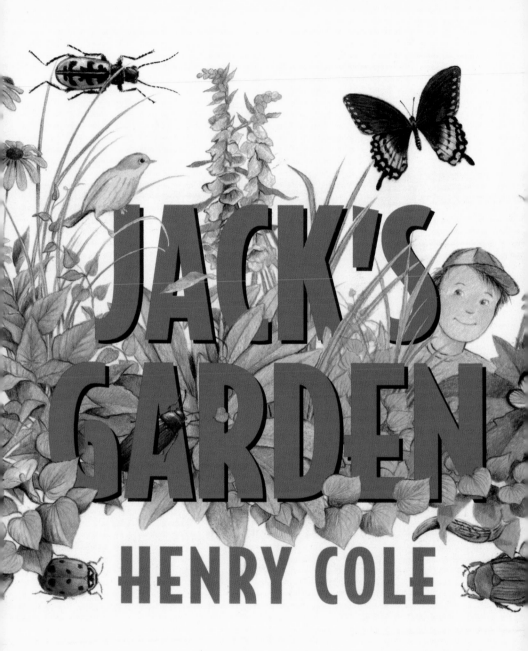

JACK'S GARDEN

HENRY COLE

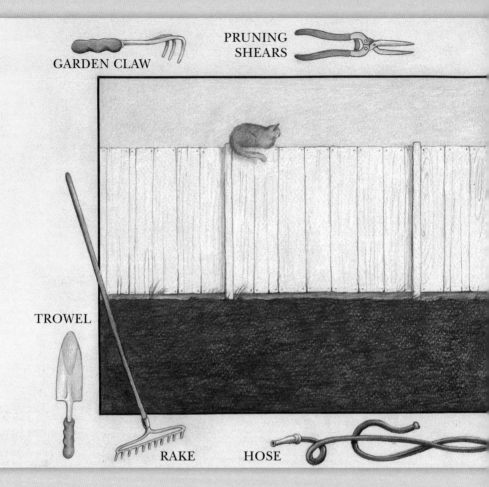

GARDEN CLAW

PRUNING SHEARS

TROWEL

RAKE HOSE

This is the garden
that Jack planted.

SHOVEL

WATERING
CAN

HOE

7

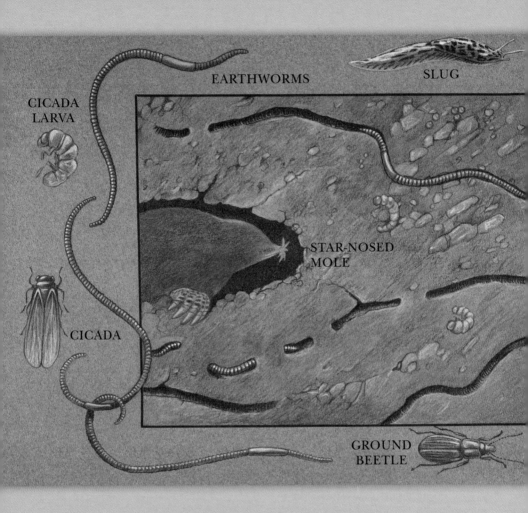

EARTHWORMS

SLUG

CICADA
LARVA

STAR-NOSED
MOLE

CICADA

GROUND
BEETLE

This is the soil

that made up the garden

that Jack planted.

FLY
PUPA

BEETLE
LARVA

SLUG EGGS

MOTH
LARVA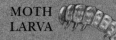

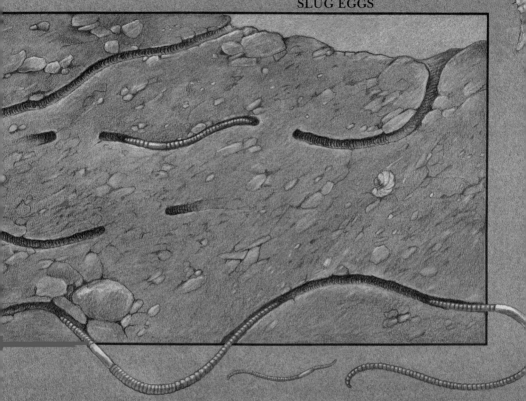

9

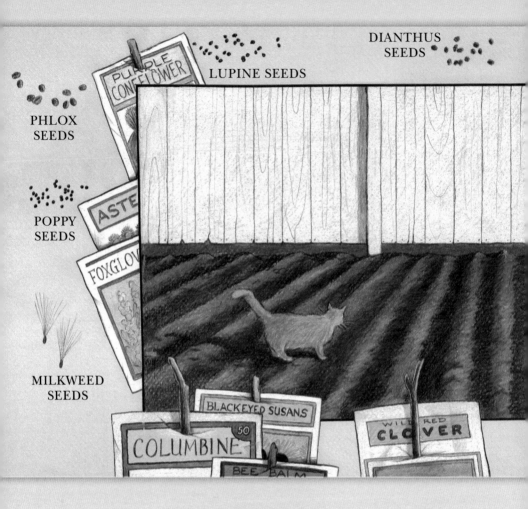

PHLOX
SEEDS

POPPY
SEEDS

MILKWEED
SEEDS

PURPLE
CONEFLOWER

ASTER

FOXGLOVE

LUPINE SEEDS

DIANTHUS
SEEDS

BLACKEYED SUSANS

COLUMBINE
50

BEE BALM

WILD RED
CLOVER

These are the seeds

that fell on the soil

that made up the garden

that Jack planted.

10

CUMULONIMBUS
CLOUD

CUMULUS
CLOUD

RAIN
GAUGE

This is the rain

that wet the seeds

that fell on the soil

that made up the garden

that Jack planted.

STRATUS CLOUD

CIRRUS CLOUD

CIRROCUMULUS CLOUD

13

SEED
LEAVES

ADULT
LEAVES

ROOTS

STEM

CENTIPEDE

MILLIPEDE

These are the seedlings
that sprouted with the rain
that wet the seeds

14

ROBIN

SOW BUG

GERMINATING
SEED

that fell on the soil

that made up the garden

that Jack planted.

15

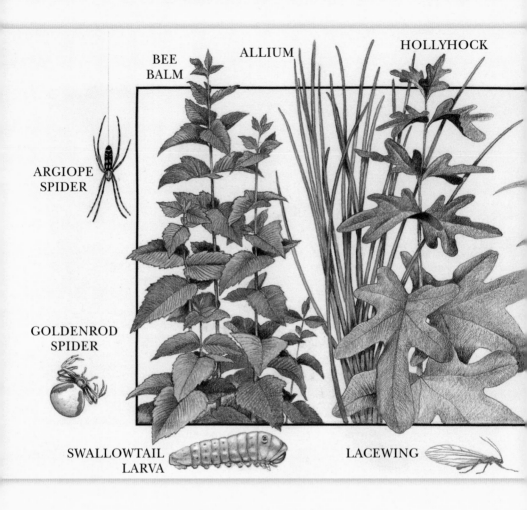

These are the plants

that grew from the seedlings

that sprouted with the rain

that wet the seeds

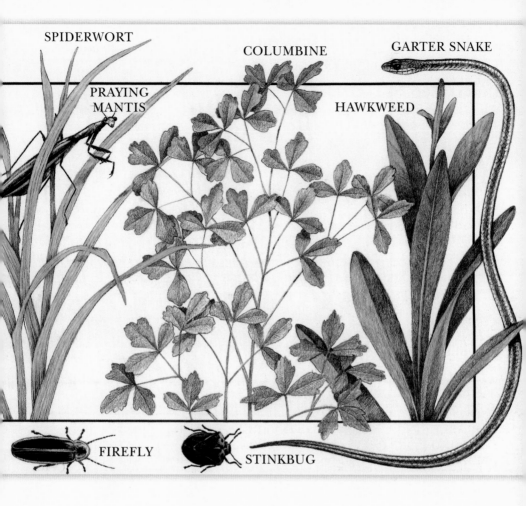

SPIDERWORT

PRAYING
MANTIS

COLUMBINE

GARTER SNAKE

HAWKWEED

FIREFLY

STINKBUG

that fell on the soil

that made up the garden

that Jack planted.

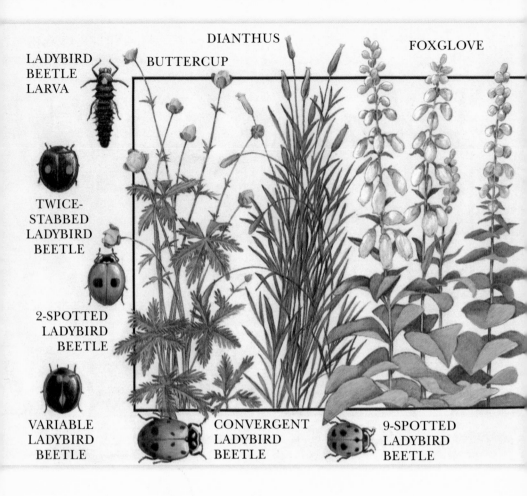

LADYBIRD BEETLE LARVA

BUTTERCUP

DIANTHUS

FOXGLOVE

TWICE-STABBED LADYBIRD BEETLE

2-SPOTTED LADYBIRD BEETLE

VARIABLE LADYBIRD BEETLE

CONVERGENT LADYBIRD BEETLE

9-SPOTTED LADYBIRD BEETLE

These are the buds

that formed on the plants

that grew from the seedlings

that sprouted with the rain

18

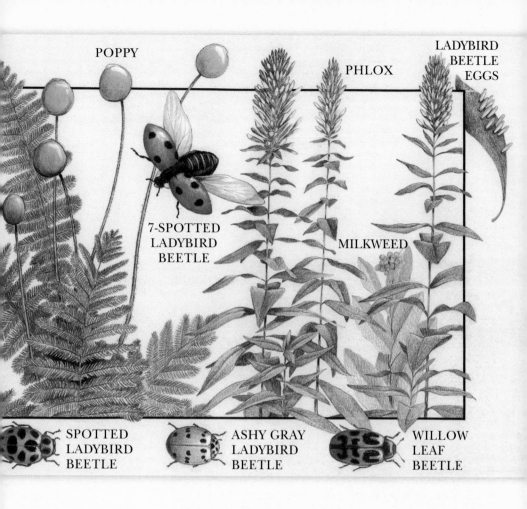

POPPY

PHLOX

LADYBIRD
BEETLE
EGGS

7-SPOTTED
LADYBIRD
BEETLE

MILKWEED

SPOTTED
LADYBIRD
BEETLE

ASHY GRAY
LADYBIRD
BEETLE

WILLOW
LEAF
BEETLE

that wet the seeds

that fell on the soil

that made up the garden

that Jack planted.

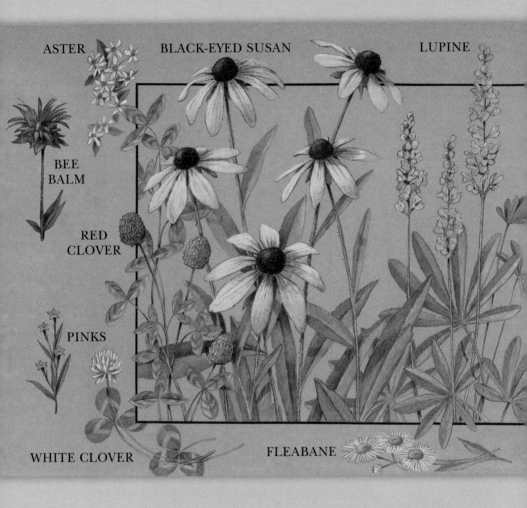

ASTER

BLACK-EYED SUSAN

LUPINE

BEE
BALM

RED
CLOVER

PINKS

WHITE CLOVER

FLEABANE

These are the flowers

that blossomed from the buds

that formed on the plants

that grew from the seedlings

that sprouted with the rain

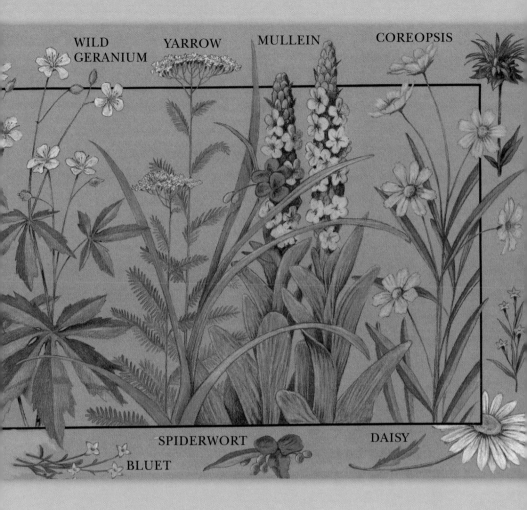

WILD GERANIUM

YARROW

MULLEIN

COREOPSIS

SPIDERWORT

BLUET

DAISY

that wet the seeds

that fell on the soil

that made up the garden

that Jack planted.

These are the insects

that sipped nectar from the flowers

that blossomed from the buds

that formed on the plants

that grew from the seedlings

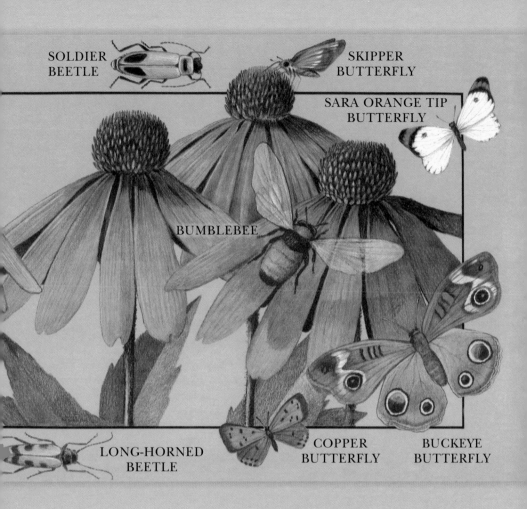

SOLDIER
BEETLE

SKIPPER
BUTTERFLY

SARA ORANGE TIP
BUTTERFLY

BUMBLEBEE

LONG-HORNED
BEETLE

COPPER
BUTTERFLY

BUCKEYE
BUTTERFLY

that sprouted with the rain

that wet the seeds

that fell on the soil

that made up the garden

that Jack planted.

23

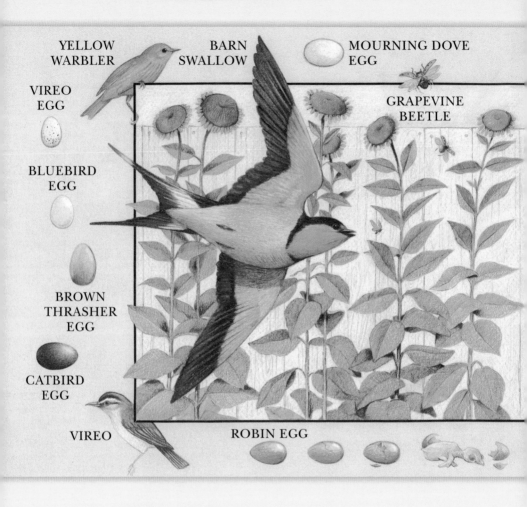

YELLOW WARBLER

BARN SWALLOW

MOURNING DOVE EGG

VIREO EGG

GRAPEVINE BEETLE

BLUEBIRD EGG

BROWN THRASHER EGG

CATBIRD EGG

VIREO

ROBIN EGG

These are the birds

that chased the insects

that sipped nectar from the flowers

that blossomed from the buds

that formed on the plants

that grew from the seedlings

YELLOW WARBLER EGG

GOLDFINCH EGG

CATBIRD

SUNFLOWERS

BLUEBIRD

BARN SWALLOW EGG

GOLDFINCH

that sprouted with the rain

that wet the seeds

that fell on the soil

that made up the garden

that Jack planted.

And this is the garden
that Jack planted.

Swirl by Swirl
Spirals in Nature

by Joyce Sidman   pictures by Beth Krommes

A spiral is a snuggling shape.
It fits neatly
        in small places.

harvest mouse

eastern chipmunk

bull snake

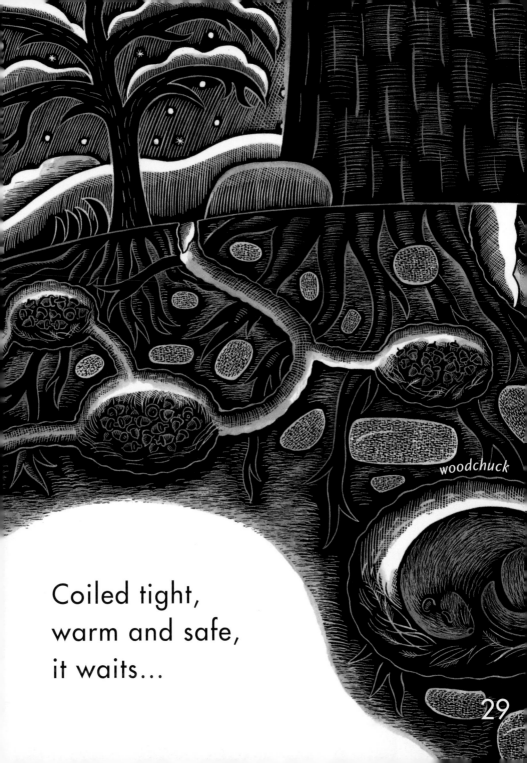

woodchuck

Coiled tight,
warm and safe,
it waits...

...for a chance to expand.

eastern chipmunk

harvest mouse

bull snake

woodchuck

A spiral is a growing shape.
It starts small
and gets bigger,

swimming nautilus

swirl
by
swirl.

cross section of nautilus shell

33

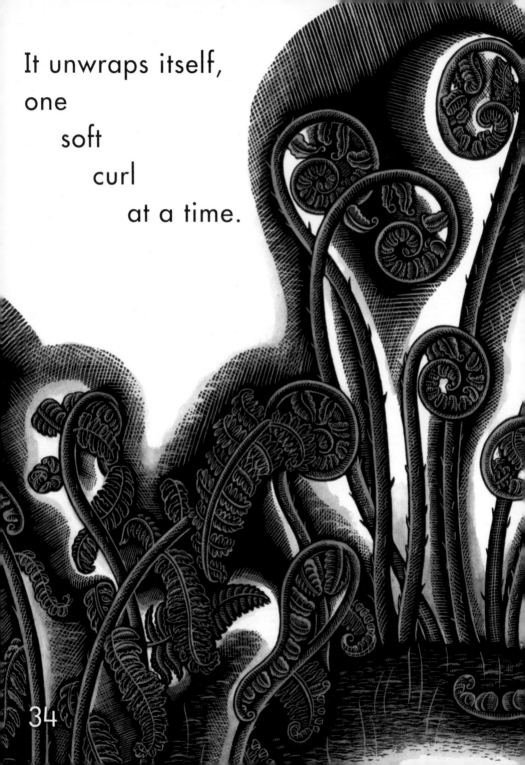

It unwraps itself,
one
   soft
      curl
         at a time.

lady fern

35

A spiral is a strong shape.

millipede

36

red fox

European hedgehog

land snail

Its outer curves
protect
what's inside.

37

It knows how
to defend itself.

merino sheep

A spiral reaches out, too, exploring the world.

common octopus

40

spiny sea horse

It winds
around
and around...

...and clings tight,
grasping what it needs.

42

spider monkey

Asian elephant

It never has trouble holding on.

43

A spiral is a clever shape.

giant swallowtail butterfly

44

garden orb spider

It is graceful and strong.

45

It is bold...

breaking ocean waves

...and beautiful.

sweet pea

daisy

angel's trumpet

rose

chrysanthemum

47

A spiral moves.

tidal whirlpool

It swirls through water,
gathering bubbles.

It twists through air

classic funnel tornado

with clouds on its tail.

It stretches starry arms
through space,

spiral galaxy

spinning and sparkling,
forever expanding…

53

eastern gray squirrel

...or, it curls up
neat and small,

*harvest
mouse*

54

warm and safe.
A spiral is a snuggling shape.

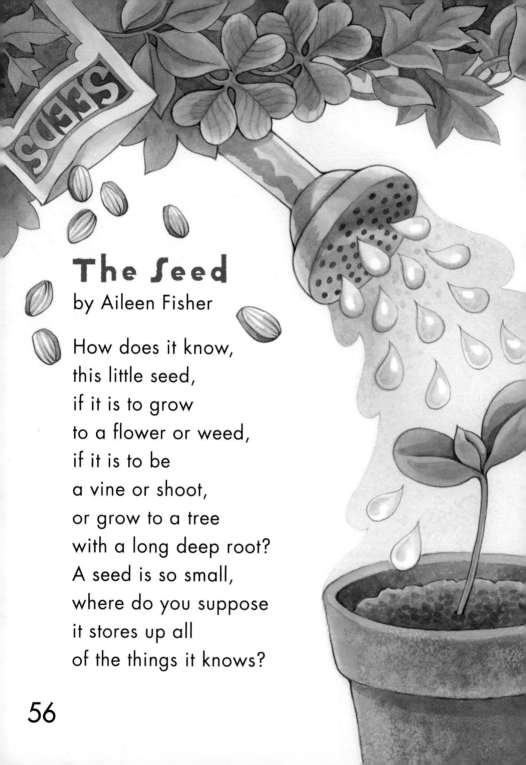

The Seed

by Aileen Fisher

How does it know,
this little seed,
if it is to grow
to a flower or weed,
if it is to be
a vine or shoot,
or grow to a tree
with a long deep root?
A seed is so small,
where do you suppose
it stores up all
of the things it knows?

Green Plants

by Meish Goldish
(sung to "Row, Row, Row Your Boat")

Grow, grow, grow your plants,
Grow with lots of care.
Carefully, carefully place your plants
Where they will get air.

Grow, grow, grow your plants,
Growing can be fun!
Carefully, carefully place your plants
Where they will get sun.

Grow, grow, grow your plants,
Never let them spoil.
Carefully, carefully place your plants
In a healthy soil.

Grow, grow, grow your plants,
One more thing to do:
Carefully, carefully give your plants
Lots of water, too!

Rainbow

by Meish Goldish
(sung to "There's a Hole in the Bucket")

There's an arc in a rainbow,
So pretty, so pretty.
There's an arc in a rainbow,
With colors you see.

The sun after rain
Makes the colors, the colors.
The sun after rain
Makes the colors you see.

58

There's red and there's orange
And there's yellow so pretty.
There's red and there's orange
And there's yellow you see.

There's green and there's blue
And there's violet so pretty.
There's green and there's blue
And there's violet you see.

There's an arc in a rainbow,
So pretty, so pretty.
There's an arc in a rainbow,
With colors you see!

Zigzag

by Loris Lesynski

zigzag here and zigzag there
see some zigzags everywhere

zigzag edges on a paper bag

fences go in a zig and zag

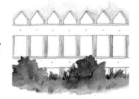

zigzag notches on a front door key

the zigzag shape of a Christmas tree

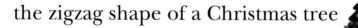

zigzag string on a basketball hoop

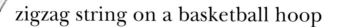

see some zigzag noodles in my soup!

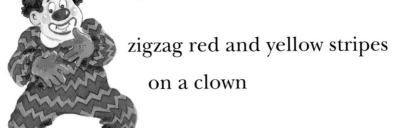

zigzag red and yellow stripes

on a clown

flashes of lightning zigzag down

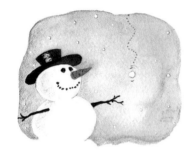

snowflakes zigzag as they fall

… and what about the bounce

what about the bounce

what about the bounce

of a Ping Pong ball?

Imagine

some bananas

in a zigzag bunch

or zigzag sandwiches

just for lunch

zigzag eyebrows?

crayons, too

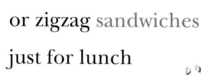

zigzag stripes on the zebra at the zoo

Up-and-down

shoulders

back-and-forth feet

get your body going

in a zigga zagga beat

zigzag elbows

zigzag toes

zigzag thumbs

… and a ziggy zaggy,

wiggle waggle,

jiggle jaggy nose

Text

Jack's Garden, by Henry Cole. Published by HarperCollins Publishers.

Swirl by Swirl: Spirals in Nature, by Joyce Sidman, illustrated by Beth Krommes. Text copyright © 2011 by Joyce Sidman. Illustrations copyright © 2011 by Beth Krommes. Reprinted by permission of Houghton Mifflin Harcourt Publishing Company. All rights reserved.

"The Seed," from *Always Wondering* by Aileen Fisher. Copyright © 1991 by Aileen Fisher. Used by permission of Marian Reiner on behalf of the Boulder Public Library Foundation, Inc.

"Green Plants," from *101 Science Poems and Songs for Young Learners* by Meish Goldish. Copyright © 1996 by Meish Goldish. Reprinted by permission of Scholastic Inc.

"Rainbow," from *101 Science Poems and Songs for Young Learners* by Meish Goldish. Copyright © 1996 by Meish Goldish. Reprinted by permission of Scholastic Inc.

"Zigzag," from *Zigzag: Zoems for Zindergarten* by Loris Lesynski. Copyright © 2004 by Loris Lesynski. Published by Annick Press Ltd. All rights reserved. Reproduced by permission.

Illustrations
56–57 Maggie Swanson, **58–59** Judith Moffatt